NIK MASANGCAY ART BOOK

WELCOME! Published and printed in 2017 by TATAY JOBO ELIZES, Self-Publisher, under the expressed permission and authorization of the author, NIK MASANGCAY, who owns the copyright to all drawings and paintings displayed in this art book. Nik Masangcay can withdraw or rescind this permission without any objection from Talay Jobo Elizes at any time. Printing of this book is using the present day method of Pnnt-On-Demand (POD) system, where prints will never run out of copies to be available for posterity. The copyright owner is free to publish his paintings with other publishers and printers anytime. ISBN Codes for this issue are:

ISBN - 13: 978 – 1547252664 & ISBN - 10: 1547252669

Contact: job elizes@yahoo.com + Websites: http://tinyurl.com/mj76ccq + www.jobelizes6.wix.com/mysite

Nik Masangcay, Acrylic in canvas, 36x24

Nik Masangcay, Acrylic in canvas, 36x24

Nic Masangcay, Dance of Faith, 48x36, acrylic in canvas

Nik Masangcay, Yakap, 14.5x21.5, watercolor

Nik Masangcay, Recollection, 8.5x11.5, inkpaper

Nik Masangcay, Darawak Falls, 14.6x10.5, watercolor

Nik Masangcay, Riverbanks, 10.5x14.5, watercolor

Nik Masangcay, San Beda Church, 29.5x21.5, watercolor

Nik Masangcay, Abstract

WELCOME! Published and printed in 2017 by TATAY JOBO ELIZES, Self-Publisher, under the expressed permission and authorization of the author, NIK MASANGCAY, who owns the copyright to all drawings and paintings displayed in this art book. Nik Masangcay can withdraw or rescind this permission without any objection from Talay Jobo Elizes at any time. Printing of this book is using the present day method of Pnnt-On-Demand (POD) system, where prints will never run out of copies to be available for posterity. The copyright owner is free to publish his paintings with other publishers and printers anytime.

Each page is suitable for framing, Just cut it out. This book is good conversation piece and for display in living rooms and coffee tables. Also good for gifts for any occasion.

Nik Masangcay, acrylic on canvas

Nik Masangcay

Nik Masangcay, Little angels

Nik Masangcay, Abstract

Nik Masangcay, Solemn ladies, acrylic on canvas

Nik Masangcay, Sabong afficionados

Nik Masangcay, Salamat Po

Nik Masangcay, Abstract Nudes study

Thank you and we hope you enjoyed this artbook. The artist can be contacted at facebook, under NIK MASANGCAY ARTHUB. He can be commissioned to do art work for you. Some of his works are available for sale. Just ask him. This book displays only 40 pieces. He has more than 200 pieces. Each page here can be cut out for framing and wall décor. This artbook is suitable for giveaway or gifts, any occasion. It's suitable for display in sala or living room and coffee table. It's perfect as conversation piece.

Nik Masangcay, Circus lady

Nik Masangcay, Sturdy bamboo trunks

Nik Masangcay, My prayer

Thank you and we hope you enjoyed this artbook. The artist can be contacted at facebook, under NIK MASANGCAY ARTHUB. He can be commissioned to do art work for you. Some of his works are available for sale. Just ask him. This book displays only 40 pieces. He has more than 200 pieces. Each page here can be cut out for framing and wall décor. This artbook is suitable for giveaway or gifts, any occasion. It's suitable for display in sala or living room and coffee table. It's perfect as conversation piece.

Nik Masangcay, A Mindanao Rani

Nik Masangcay with co-artist Calata, Xmas Carols

Nik Masangcay, 45x30, Queen of Hearts, acrylic

Nik Masangcay, Orchid

Nik Masangcay, modern ladies

Thank you and we hope you enjoyed this artbook. The artist can be contacted at facebook, under NIK MASANGCAY ARTHUB. He can be commissioned to do art work for you. Some of his works are available for sale. Just ask him. This book displays only 40 pieces. He has more than 200 pieces. Each page here can be cut out for framing and wall décor.

Nik Masangcay, Mother and child

Nik Masangcay, Christmas season

Thank you and we hope you enjoyed this artbook. The artist can be contacted at facebook, under NIK MASANGCAY ARTHUB. He can be commissioned to do art work for you. Some of his works are available for sale. Just ask him. This book displays only 40 pieces. He has more than 200 pieces. Each page here can be cut out for framing and wall décor. This artbook is suitable for giveaway or gifts, any occasion. It's suitable for display in sala or living room and coffee table. It's perfect as conversation piece.

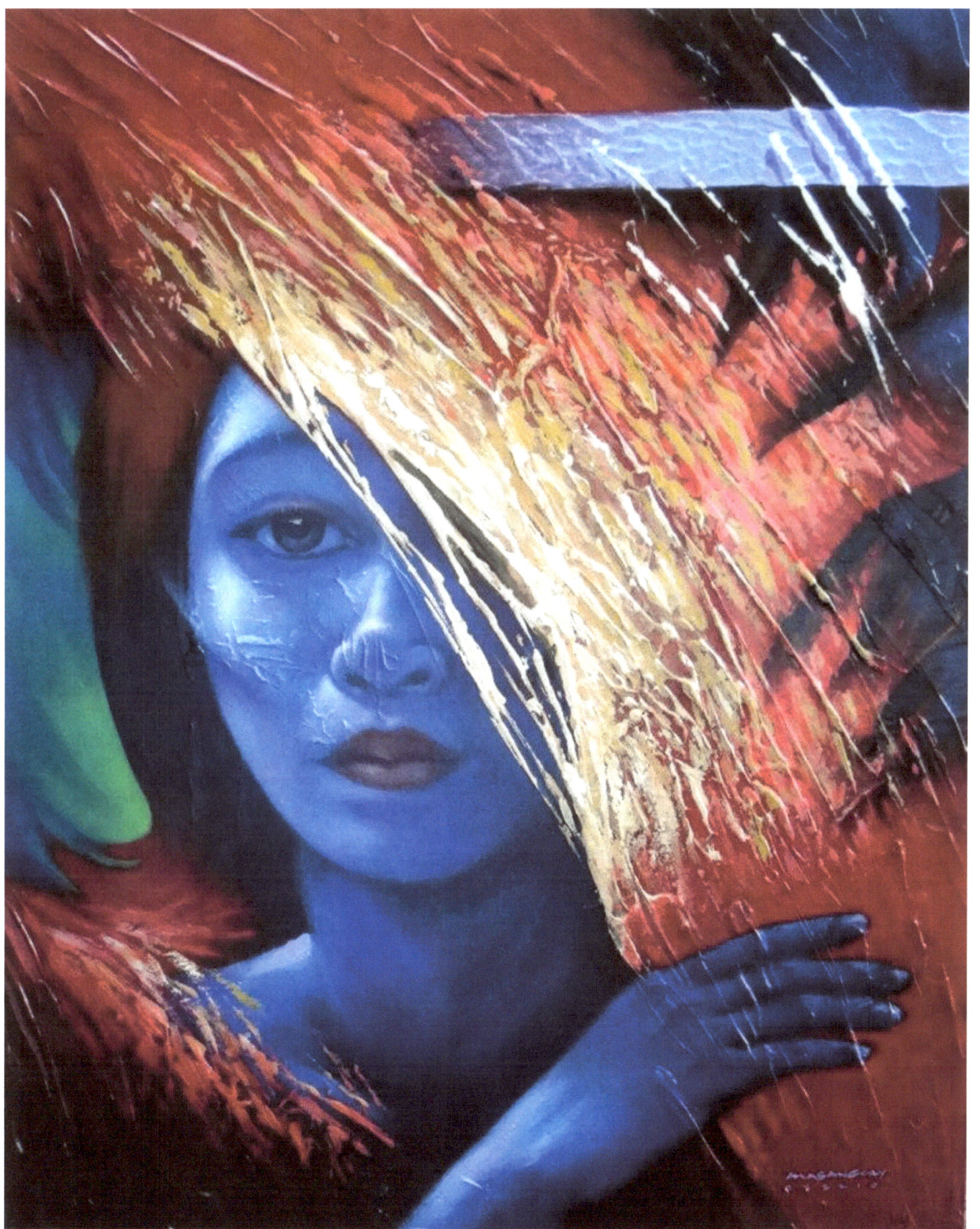

Nik Masangcay, Shy lady

Nik Masangcay, Feelin d blues, 24x24, acrylic

Thank you and we hope you enjoyed this artbook. The artist can be contacted at facebook, under NIK MASANGCAY ARTHUB. He can be commissioned to do art work for you. Some of his works are available for sale. Just ask him. This book displays only 40 pieces. He has more than 200 pieces. Each page here can be cut out for framing and wall décor. This artbook is suitable for giveaway or gifts, any occasion. It's suitable for display in sala or living room and coffee table. It's perfect as conversation piece.

Nik Masangcay, Ibahay, ati-ati, 24x24, acrylic

Thank you and we hope you enjoyed this artbook. The artist can be contacted at facebook, under NIK MASANGCAY ARTHUB. He can be commissioned to do art work for you. Some of his works are available for sale. Just ask him. This book displays only 40 pieces. He has more than 200 pieces. Each page here can be cut out for framing and wall décor. This artbook is suitable for giveaway or gifts, any occasion. It's suitable for display in sala or living room and coffee table. It's perfect as conversation piece.

Thank you and we hope you enjoyed this artbook. The artist can be contacted at facebook, under NIK MASANGCAY ARTHUB. He can be commissioned to do art work for you. Some of his works are available for sale. Just ask him. This book displays only 40 pieces. He has more than 200 pieces. Each page here can be cut out for framing and wall décor. This artbook is suitable for giveaway or gifts, any occasion. It's suitable for display in sala or living room and coffee table. It's perfect as conversation piece.

Nik Masangcay, Lie low

Nik Masangcay, Guiarist

Nik Masangcay, Scary abstract

Nik Masangcay, Nanay at Anak

Nik Masangcay, Symbolic Logo

Nik Masangcay, Patient ladies

Nik Masangcay, Lonesome lady

Thank you and we hope you enjoyed this artbook. The artist can be contacted at facebook, under NIK MASANGCAY ARTHUB. He can be commissioned to do art work for you. Some of his works are available for sale. Just ask him. This book displays only 40 pieces. He has more than 200 pieces. Each page here can be cut out for framing and wall décor. This artbook is suitable for giveaway or gifts, any occasion. It's suitable for display in sala or living room and coffee table. It's perfect as conversation piece.

Nik Masangcay, Fruit Vendor

Thank you and we hope you enjoyed this artbook. The artist can be contacted at facebook, under NIK MASANGCAY ARTHUB. He can be commissioned to do art work for you. Some of his works are available for sale. Just ask him. This book displays only 40 pieces. He has more than 200 pieces. Each page here can be cut out for framing and wall décor. This artbook is suitable for giveaway or gifts, any occasion. It's suitable for display in sala or living room and coffee table. It's perfect as conversation piece.

Nik Masangcay, bird feeding

Nik Masangkay, Nanay and Neneng

Thank you and we hope you enjoyed this artbook.
The artist can be contacted at facebook, under
NIK MASANGCAY ARTHUB
He can be commissioned to do art work for you.
Some of his works are available for sale. Just ask him.
This book displays only 40 pieces. He has more than 200 pieces.
Each page here can be cut out for framing and wall décor.
This artbook is suitable for giveaway or gifts, any occasion.
It's suitable for display in sala or living room and coffee table.
It's perfect as conversation piece.

Maraming salamat po.

www.ingramcontent.com/pod-product-compliance
Lightning Source LLC
Chambersburg PA
CBHW051105180526
45172CB00002B/789